Poetry is NOT for me!

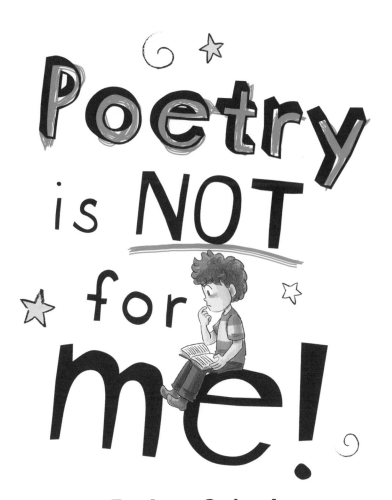

Poetry is NOT for me!

Joshua Seigal

Illustrated by
Rebecca Burgess

Collins

Contents

Chapter 1 In class. 3

Chapter 2 Asking Dad 10

Chapter 3 Asking Jess 21

Chapter 4 Asking Mum 29

Chapter 5 Making the poem. 39

Chapter 6 Back in class 49

Damon's edits 58

Joshua's top poetry writing tips . . 60

Noisy words. 62

Repetition 64

Ode. 66

Short poems 68

About the author 70

About the illustrator 72

Book chat 74

Chapter 1
In class

The last day of term was warm and sunny, but Damon was feeling bored. His teacher, Mrs Bloom, was talking about something called *poetry*.

"A poem," Mrs Bloom said, "is a little piece of writing where you need to use your imagination." She went on to explain, "Poems can be about anything you like. Sometimes they can rhyme, but they don't have to."

Damon felt a sense of fatigue. He could not
concentrate on what Mrs Bloom was saying.
He looked out of the window, and saw a bird
perched on a branch. Damon felt he would much
rather be outside in the sun.

Mrs Bloom said that everyone would be writing
a poem for homework over the holidays.
Hearing this, Damon began to feel nervous.
He didn't think he would be able to write a poem.
In fact, he was sure that he wouldn't. He'd never
written a poem before.

Poetry is not for me, Damon thought. These words kept going round and round in his head: *Poetry is not for me! Poetry is not for me!*

The words ran through his brain for the rest of the day, until it was time to go home — *Poetry is not for me!* Then, just before home time, Mrs Bloom noticed that Damon looked agitated. She took him aside.

"Is everything OK?" Mrs Bloom asked.

"It's the poem," Damon said. "I don't think I can do it."

"Don't worry, Damon!" said Mrs Bloom. "You can do wonderful things if you put your mind to it! Everyone feels nervous about doing new things sometimes."

Mrs Bloom pulled her bag towards her.

"I've got something that might help with your poem," she said. She gave Damon a notebook. The notebook was shiny and red, and looked very new.

"Whenever you get an idea," Mrs Bloom continued, "just write it down in this notebook. You mustn't worry if the ideas don't come at first – just write whatever comes into your mind. Have a routine and write something every day, even if it's just something small."

Damon held the notebook tightly.

"Remember," said Mrs Bloom, "a poem can be about anything you like."

Later that evening, Damon sat in his room staring at the notebook he had received. He was still feeling worried. He didn't want to write a poem; all he wanted to do was to be free like the birds. Those words were still going round in his head — *Poetry is not for me!* Then Damon had an idea: he decided that he would write in his notebook.

He took a pencil, and this is what he wrote:

Poetry is not for me

I'd rather be outside and free.

Chapter 2
Asking Dad

Next morning, Damon woke up with a vague feeling that something was wrong. This was because he was still very worried about writing his poem. He heard noises coming from the garden, so he looked out of the window. Dad was out there, doing some gardening in the sunshine.

Damon rushed outside and went up to his dad.

"Dad," said Damon, "will you help me write a poem?"

"Sorry," Dad replied with a gentle smile. "I'm far too busy watering the lawn. If I don't water it in this warm weather, the grass won't grow."

The sun was blazing down in the garden, and the sky was blue. There were just a few faint, tufty clouds floating slowly above them. Damon wished that the inside of his mind was free and open, like the sky. If his mind was like the sky, Damon thought, he would be able to fill it with ideas.

It might have been summertime outside, but Damon felt that, inside himself, it was like winter. If only he could water his ideas like Dad was watering the grass. That way, his ideas would be able to grow, too.

Damon sat down on a step. Noticing that Damon was looking worried, Dad turned off the garden hose and came to sit next to him.

"What's wrong, Damon?" he asked.

"It's the poem," Damon said. "I don't think I can do it."

Dad put his arm around his son.

"If you put your mind to it," Dad said soothingly, "I guarantee you will be surprised at what you come up with." Damon tried to smile, but it was a very weak smile indeed. Inside, he still felt bleak and wintry.

"But why won't you help me?" Damon asked.

Dad replied that he needed to help the grass.

"You are big and brave and powerful," Dad said.
"The grass needs my help more than you do."

Damon didn't feel big and brave and powerful.
He felt weak, like the thirsty grass.

That evening, Damon opened up his notebook again. He thought about what Dad had said, about helping the grass to grow. Damon still felt nervous about writing his poem, but he felt that he had just enough confidence to pick up his pencil and write something down.

Damon added these words to the words he had
written the previous day:

I asked Dad for help

But Dad told me no.

He was watering the grass

So he could help it grow.

He put his notebook away with a sigh. He was glad
he had written something small, but it still felt as
though writing a whole poem was something he
couldn't do. How would he ever get this poem done?
Worry continued to flow through his veins, and
Damon climbed wearily into bed.

Chapter 3
Asking Jess

Damon was woken the following day by a clattering sound coming from the room next door.

Of course, thought Damon, *I'll ask my big sister Jess for help with my poem!*

He went into her messy room. She was extremely busy clunking around, trying to clear away all her toys.

"Jess," said Damon, "will you help me write my poem?"

"Sorry," replied Jess. "My room is really very untidy. Mum says that if I don't clean it, I won't get any pocket money!"

It was no use. Jess clearly wouldn't be able to help Damon either.

Damon watched as Jess seized a pile of toys and clothes and put them away. She picked up a pair of jeans that were lying on the floor, and she folded them and placed them on a shelf in her wardrobe. After that, she grabbed hold of some soft toys that lay scattered about. She arranged them neatly on her bed.

Damon noticed that, as Jess was tidying her room, the floor was becoming clearer. Now instead of being covered with toys, Damon could begin to see the carpet underneath. The mess on the floor reminded him of his own worries that were littering his mind. He wished he could clear them away, just like Jess was clearing up her room.

As Damon was sulkily walking towards the door, Jess called him back.

"What's wrong?" she asked. She could see that Damon was looking glum.

"Mrs Bloom says I have to write a poem," Damon murmured, "but I don't think I'll be able to do it."

Jess smiled kindly and put her arm around him, just as Dad had done.

"You're my unique little brother," Jess replied.
"You can do whatever you put your mind to.
I guarantee it. Anyway," she went on, "these toys
and clothes won't clear themselves away. They're
smaller than you, and they need me more than
you do."

Damon managed a smile, but he still felt small and
helpless, like the toys in Jess's room.

After tea, Damon continued the routine of taking out his notebook. His chat with Jess had made him feel a little bit better. He felt that some of his worries had been cleared away, but only a little bit. He was still disappointed that Jess would not help with his poem.

Despite the fact that he was feeling worried, he did feel brave enough do a little bit more writing.

This is what he wrote down:

I asked for help

From my big sister Jess,

But she said she was too busy

Because her bedroom was a mess.

Damon put his notebook away and crawled under his covers. He lay there for what seemed like hours. How would he ever be able to write a whole poem?

Chapter 4
Asking Mum

Damon came down the stairs the next morning and the gloomy feeling had returned. Whilst he was pleased that he had managed to write a bit in his notebook, he was still upset because no one was able to help him with his poem.

Damon's mum was busy decorating the kitchen wall.

"Mum," asked Damon, "will you help me write my poem? Mrs Bloom said I need to write a poem over the holidays, but I don't think I can do it."

Damon's mum was at the top of a very tall ladder.

"I'm sorry Damon," she said. "I'd love to help, but I'm far too busy doing this decorating."

Mum was painting over the wall with dazzling green strokes of paint. The wall underneath was a dull beige colour, which Mum was gradually covering, bit by bit, with her thick green stripes. The beige colour of the wall reminded Damon of his anxiety. If only he had his own special paint, so that he could paint over all his worries about the poem, to make them disappear.

As Damon watched Mum applying layers and layers of lovely green paint to the dull beige wall, Damon pictured his worries disappearing. His stomach, which had felt tense all week, gradually started to feel a bit better.

Damon considered discussing his worries a bit more with Mum, like he had done with Dad and with Jess. He also considered begging Mum one more time for help with his poem. However, he had a feeling that if he did, she'd just tell him that the kitchen wall needed her help more than he did! Damon smiled softly and left the kitchen.

The sky that night was dark and clear, and filled with stars. Were they shining just for him? Damon could hear what sounded like an owl hooting off in the distance. Was it calling to him? He took out his notebook and, just as he had done the previous evenings, put his pencil to the paper.

This is what he wrote:

Mum can't help me.

She can't help me at all.

She's busy in the kitchen

And she's painting the wall.

Damon shut the notebook and looked at the cover.

He noticed very vague swirls in amongst
the red background. The faint swirls reminded him
of his feelings, sometimes going up and sometimes
going down, wiggling and winding in many
different directions.

"Isn't it funny," Damon thought, "how I can feel hopeful one minute and then worried the next? Perhaps that's just what happens when you try to write poetry. Perhaps that's just part of life."

The stars glimmered and the owl hooted. The swirls on the cover of Damon's notebook went round and round with their mysterious patterns.

Chapter 5
Making the poem

Damon felt glad that his family believed in him, but he was also worried that he hadn't managed to write the poem that Mrs Bloom had asked him to. He sat on the edge of his bed, looking at the words in his notebook once more.

This is what he had written down:

Poetry is not for me.

I'd rather be outside and free.

I asked Dad for help

But Dad told me no.

He was watering the grass

So he could help it grow.

I asked for help

From my big sister Jess,

But she said she was too busy

Because her bedroom was a mess.

Mum can't help me.

She can't help me at all.

She's busy in the kitchen

And she's painting the wall.

Suddenly, Damon thought back to what
Mrs Bloom had said in class. She said a poem
can be about anything you like. She also said that
poems can sometimes rhyme. Damon read over his
words again, and a miraculous lightbulb seemed to
flash in his mind.

Wow! thought Damon with wonder. *Maybe I have
written a poem after all!*

Damon began to feel very proud of himself.
He realised that, although he had been nervous at
first, he was actually a very good writer. His mind
had grown, just like the grass. He had cleared
away some of the mess inside it, just like the toys
in Jess's room. He had gently overcome some of his
anxiety, just like Mum had covered the wall with
new paint in the kitchen.

Damon decided to read over what he had written.
He looked again at the language he had used, and
he made little changes here and there. He took some
of the words away, and he also swapped some of
the words around.

Damon remembered that Mrs Bloom had explained that there is a word for this: "editing". Damon edited his poem until he was really happy with how the words sounded.

Beaming with pride, he then added a final verse to his poem:

My smile is wide!

My mind is blown!

I wrote this poem

On my own!

He was very excited to show Mrs Bloom and the rest of the class what he had written.

Over the next few days, Damon practised reading his poem. He looked at himself in the mirror and read his poem in funny voices. He read it squeakily, like a hamster, and he read it gruffly, like a dinosaur. He performed it in a whole range of hilarious ways.

He read it whilst spinning around and whilst standing on his head. He read it in the bath and he even read it on the toilet! He read it over and over again, practising and practising. Damon felt exhilarated; he was really enjoying the experience!

Chapter 6
Back in class

It was the end of the holidays, and everyone
was back in class. The beautiful weather had
turned to rain, which fell down in columns across
the playground. The sun, which had been shining
so brightly, was extinguished. However, Damon did
not mind. His heart was filled with sunshine.

Mrs Bloom asked if anyone would like to share
the poem they had written over the holidays.
She explained that, when reading out a poem,
it is best to read it slowly, in a loud, clear voice,
so that everyone can hear all the words.
Damon felt confident. His hand shot up at once.

He went to the front of the class, with a wide smile beaming on his face. He read the title of his poem in a nice, loud, clear voice:

Poetry Is Not For Me

Then he read out the poem he had worked so hard
to edit:

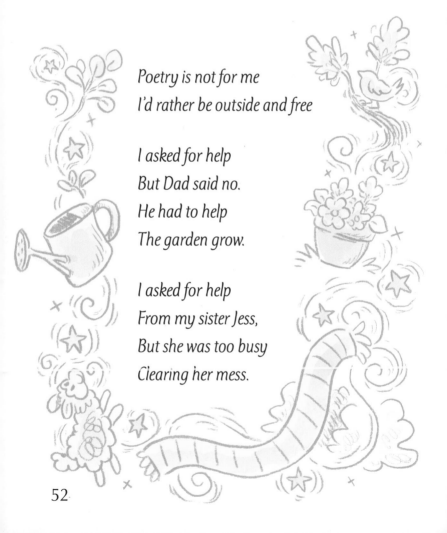

Poetry is not for me
I'd rather be outside and free

I asked for help
But Dad said no.
He had to help
The garden grow.

I asked for help
From my sister Jess,
But she was too busy
Clearing her mess.

Mum can't help me,
Not at all.
She's busy painting
The kitchen wall.

My smile is wide!
My mind is blown!
I wrote this poem
On my own!

53

Everybody clapped, and Damon swelled with pride at what he had accomplished. He had written his very own poem!

"Well done, Damon," said Mrs Bloom with a grin on her face.

Some of the other children stood up and read their poems too. There were poems about all kinds of different things. Mina read a poem about her pet rabbit, and Anton read a poem about football.

All the poems used different techniques. Some of the poems were long, and some of them were short. Some of them had a strong rhythm. Some of them rhymed, like Damon's, but others didn't. One of the poems that didn't rhyme was Mrs Bloom's.

"Since you all wrote a poem over the holidays," Mrs Bloom said, "I thought I should write one too!"

Mrs Bloom explained that writing the poem made her feel nervous at first, but when she put her mind to it, she started to enjoy the process.

She stood up, and in a lovely, clear voice, this is what she read out:

You Can Do Anything

You can do anything
if you put your mind to it

You can do more than you think

You can reach out into the sky
and pluck a star from the night

You can slide down a rainbow
or dance on a cloud

You can go exploring
in the jaws of a dreadful dragon

You can gather the notes of a song
and the spark of an idea

You can do anything
If you put your mind to it

You can do more than you think

You can even
Write a poem ...

Damon's edits

Poetry is not for me
I'd rather be outside and free

I asked ~~Dad~~ for help
But Dad ~~told me~~ said no.
~~He was watering the grass~~ He had to help
~~So he could help it grow~~ The garden grow.

I asked for help
From my ~~big~~ sister Jess,
But she ~~said she~~ was too busy
~~Because her bedroom was a mess~~
Clearing her mess.

Mum can't help me,
~~She can't help me at all~~ Not at all.
She's busy ~~in the kitchen~~ painting
~~And she's painting the wall~~ The kitchen wall.

My smile is wide!
My mind is blown!
I wrote this poem
On my own!

Joshua's top poetry writing tips

Hello everyone! Joshua here (I'm a poet and the author of this book). Did you know, you can write your very own poem! Here are some of my top tips for writing your own poetry.

Try and read lots of different poems.

Remember: poems do not have to rhyme.

Like Damon, try to get into the routine of writing a little bit every day.

Write about things that you're interested in.

When you think you've finished your poem, go back and do some editing. Think about the words you have used – are they the best words for the job? Are there different words you could use instead?

Keep a notebook, just like Damon. Whenever you get an idea, jot it down.

Practise reading your poem out loud. You can read it in lots of different ways, like Damon.

This is the most important tip … HAVE FUN!!!!!

Noisy words

This poem of mine uses "noisy" words.

My Kitten Goes "Moo"
by Joshua Seigal

My kitten goes "MOO"

and my snake says "MEEOW".

My donkey goes "HISS"

and "HEE-HAW" says my cow.

My rabbit goes "RIBBIT".

My horses say "CLUCK".

My penguin goes "ROAR"

and "AWOOO" says my duck.

My chicken goes "BUZZ"

and my hamster says "NEIGH".

My octopus TWITTERS

and CHIRRUPS all day.

It's all quite confusing –

"BOW-WOW" says my crow

while my sister just CLUCKS

as my hen says "HELLO!"

Now try writing a poem using lots of noisy words.

Repetition

This poem uses something called repetition – every verse begins with the same words.

Lucky Pants
by Joshua Seigal

Lucky pants

Wear them tight

Lucky pants

Feel just right

Lucky pants

Blue and red

Lucky pants

On my head

Lucky pants

While I sleep

Lucky pants

Mine to keep!

You can now try writing your own poem like this. It can rhyme, but only if you want! It can also be a bit silly, like mine.

Ode

An ode is a poem in praise of a special person. I wrote this one for my grandma.

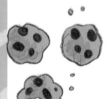

Great Grandma
by Joshua Seigal

Whenever I go over

she has cookies on a plate.

She lets me watch TV shows

and she lets me stay up late.

She's got a little fluffy cat.

She bakes some tasty treats,

then tucks me up in bed at night

in comfy, cosy sheets.

I love to go and stay at hers

and see her beaming face.

I think she's my "great grandma"

as she's really, really ace.

Why not have a go at writing a poem about someone special to you? It can rhyme, like mine, but again – only if you want!

Short poems

These poems have just three lines.
The first line has five syllables;
the second line has seven syllables
and the final line has five syllables.

Summer
by Joshua Seigal

The sun smiles softly.

Blades of grass sway in the breeze.

A sparrow takes flight.

Winter
by Joshua Seigal

Snow blankets the path.

Inside we're huddled and warm

As angry winds blow.

Short poems usually do not rhyme. They are often about nature. Why not try writing your own?

About the author

How did you get into writing?

I've always loved words! I wrote lots of stories and poems when I was little, and I never really stopped. I try to do lots of reading too, as this is an excellent way of getting inspiration.

Joshua Seigal

What do you hope readers will get out of the book?

I hope readers will come away feeling that they can have a go at writing some poetry of their own! It can be a very enjoyable thing to do.

Is there anything in this book that relates to your own experiences?

Like Damon, I sometimes find it hard to think of ideas, and like Damon, ideas sometimes come from unexpected places.

What is it like for you to write?

It is very enjoyable, but it can also be challenging. It involves a whole mixture of emotions!

What is a book you remember loving reading when you were young?

I loved *The Twits*. And I've always been mesmerised by atlases.

Are any of the characters based on people you know in real life?

I had a wonderful teacher when I was at school, so I suppose Mrs Bloom might be based on her. My dad also likes gardening, like Damon's dad!

In the story, Damon doesn't get writing help from his family. Do you think that's a good thing?

Interesting question! I think it's good to help people when they need it, but sometimes the best help can be showing people they can be independent.

How do you get inspiration for your poetry? Is there anything that you would not write a poem about?

I get inspiration from anywhere and everywhere, but I would never, ever, EVER, write a poem about guinea pigs!!

About the illustrator

A bit about me …

I live in Bristol and like gardening and going on adventures to explore the local wildlife. When I'm not outdoors, I really like cuddling my cat and building models.

Rebecca Burgess

What made you want to be an illustrator?

I don't think I had a choice. I've been drawing for as long as I could pick up a pencil, and have drawn one picture every day since I was twelve!

How did you get into illustration?

When I was thirteen I started making and printing out my own comics, and selling those at comic conventions! That way I made lots of friends who made comics and they helped to get me jobs.

What did you like best about illustrating this book?

I like drawing feelings best. Damon had a lot of emotions to draw.

What was the most difficult thing about illustrating this book?

Colouring the drawings was hard, I'm not naturally very good at picking out which colours to use, and have to work extra hard to make sure I get them right.

Is there anything in this book that relates to your own experiences?

Just like Damon, I also tend to overthink things and worry until the worrying takes over everything. But also just like Damon, I normally try to confront my worrying in little steps, and very soon I find I'm happy again!

How do you bring a character to life?

I make lots of small doodles first in a sketch book to work out a character's personality. Then I draw the line art with pencils, then scan that into my laptop and colour the drawings digitally.

Do you ever base the characters you draw on people you know in real life?

All the time! When I'm drawing crowds where you draw lots of people, I like to draw film characters too.

Book chat

If you could ask the author one question, what would it be?

If you had to give the book a new title, what would you choose?

If you could have a conversation with one character from the book, who would you pick? What would you say to them?

Did this book make you want to try writing your own poems?

Do you think Damon changed between the start of the story and the end? If so, how?

If you had to pick one scene to act out, which would you choose? Why?

Did this book remind you of anything you have experienced in real life?

Do you think it was good that Damon's family didn't help him with his poem?

How do you think Damon felt at the end of the story? How would you feel if you were him?

Book challenge:

Have a go at making up your own poem. You could work with someone else and take turns to say a line.

Collins
BIG CAT

Published by Collins
An imprint of HarperCollins*Publishers*

The News Building
1 London Bridge Street
London SE1 9GF
UK

Macken House
39/40 Mayor Street Upper
Dublin 1
D01 C9W8
Ireland

British Library Cataloguing-in-Publication Data
A catalogue record for this publication is available
from the British Library.

Download the teaching notes and
word cards to accompany this book at:
http://littlewandle.org.uk/signupfluency/

Get the latest Collins Big Cat news at
collins.co.uk/collinsbigcat

Author: Joshua Seigal
Illustrator: Rebecca Burgess
Publisher: Lizzie Catford
Product manager and
   commissioning editor: Caroline Green
Series editor: Charlotte Raby
Development editor: Catherine Baker
Project manager: Emily Hooton
Content editor: Daniela Mora Chavarría
Copy editor: Catherine Dakin
Phonics reviewer: Rachel Russ
Proofreader: Gaynor Spry
Cover designer: Sarah Finan
Designer: 2Hoots Publishing Services Ltd
Production controller: Katharine Willard

Collins would like to thank the teachers and
children at the following schools who took part in
the trialling of Big Cat for Little Wandle Fluency:
Burley And Woodhead Church of England Primary
School; Chesterton Primary School; Lady Margaret
Primary School; Little Sutton Primary School;
Parsloes Primary School.

Printed and bound in the UK by Page Bros Group Ltd

MIX
Paper | Supporting
responsible forestry
FSC™ C007454

This book is produced from independently
certified FSC™ paper to ensure
responsible forest management.

For more information visit:
www.harpercollins.co.uk/green